What are you

CHAPTER TWO
Fast and Forceful
PAGE **10**

CHAPTER ONE
Rising Water
PAGE **4**

curious about?

CHAPTER THREE

Water Watches
PAGE **18**

Stay Curious! Learn More . . .22
Glossary. 24
Index 24

Curious About is published by
Amicus Learning, an imprint of Amicus
P.O. Box 227, Mankato, MN 56002
www.amicuspublishing.us

Copyright © 2026 Amicus.
International copyright reserved in all countries.
No part of this book may be reproduced in any
form without written permission from the publisher.

Editor: Ana Brauer
Series Designer: Kathleen Petelinsek
Book Designer and Photo Researcher: Sara Hood

Library of Congress Cataloging-in-Publication Data
Names: Koestler-Grack, Rachel A., 1973– author
Title: Curious about floods / by Rachel Grack.
Description: Mankato, MN : Amicus Learning, an imprint of
Amicus, [2026] | Series: Curious about extreme weather |
Includes bibliographical references and index. | Audience:
Ages 6–9 | Audience: Grades 2–3 | Summary: "Where
do floods happen? Learn the causes and effects of one of
nature's most common disasters in this question-and-answer
book for elementary-aged readers. Includes infographics,
table of contents, glossary, books and websites for further
research, and index"— Provided by publisher.
Identifiers: LCCN 2025012819 (print) | LCCN 2025012820
(ebook) | ISBN 9798892008389 library binding | ISBN
9798892009041 paperback | ISBN 9798892009706 ebook
Subjects: LCSH: Floods—Juvenile literature
Classification: LCC GB1399 .K64 2026 (print) | LCC GB1399
(ebook) | DDC 551.48/9—dc23/eng/20250728
LC record available at https://lccn.loc.gov/2025012819
LC ebook record available at https://lccn.loc.gov/2025012820

Photo Credits: Alamy Stock Photo/Adrian Sherratt, 3, 18–19,
Thierry Cariou, cover, 1; Getty Images/ArtMarie, 2, 9 (second
from bottom), CFOTO, 8, Luis Diaz Devesa, 2, 16–17, MARK
GARLICK/SCIENCE PHOTO LIBRARY, 12, Paul Smaldone,
14, Photography by Mangiwau, 13, Vishal Bhatnagar/
NurPhoto, 9 (bottom); Shutterstock/AlinaMD, 9 (top), Bilanol,
5, Evannovostro, 6–7, Golden Sikorka, 21, Graphic toons,
21, kamran kami, 10–11, Macrovector, 21, Mundofoto, 9
(second from top), Sunbeam_ks, 21, TFoxFoto, 20, Vectorbum,
21, Victoruler, 21, Zaporizhzhia vector, 15; The Noun
Project/El Hikami, 22, 23, metami septiana, 22, 23

Every effort has been made to contact copyright holders for
material reproduced in this book. Any omissions will be rectified
in subsequent printings if notice is given to the publisher.

Printed in United States of America

CHAPTER ONE

What are floods?

Floods happen when water flows onto dry land. The floodwater can be just a few inches (centimeters) deep. Or it may cover the rooftops of houses. Floods take place almost anywhere and at any time of year. They are the most common natural disaster. But some are caused by humans.

DID YOU KNOW?
The Johnstown Flood of 1889 had both natural and human causes. Heavy rain caused a dam in Pennsylvania to burst.

Floodwaters can cover roads and make driving dangerous.

RISING WATER

RISING WATER

Which floods are caused by humans?

A broken dam is a common cause of human-made floods.

Those caused by mistakes. These floods can be worse than natural floods. One of the deadliest floods in history was started on purpose. In 1938, Chinese soldiers broke **dikes** to flood the path of Japanese troops. Water gushed out of control. Floodwaters killed more than 800,000 people.

River floods are common in many places around the world, such as China.

What causes natural floods?

That depends on the type. Rivers often flood after days of rain. Melting snow also causes river flooding. **Storm surges** flood coasts during hurricanes and tropical storms. Flash floods are the most dangerous.

RIVER FLOOD
BANKS OVERFLOW

FLASH FLOOD
HIGH AMOUNTS OF RAIN

STORM SURGE
COASTAL FLOOD

URBAN FLOOD
CITY DRAINS OVERFLOW

FLOOD TYPES

CHAPTER TWO

What are flash floods?

Floods that hit very suddenly. They catch people off guard. Flash floods can strike when there is heavy rainfall. They happen faster on hard or rocky ground. Mountains and steep hills speed up **runoff**. A downpour sends water rushing downhill. It can cause a flash flood miles (kilometers) away.

Flash floods usually happen without warning.

DID YOU KNOW?
Floating chunks of ice can cause ice jams on rivers. Water builds up until the jam finally breaks. Whoosh! Flash flood!

Can an earthquake cause a flood?

Yes! The shaking ground can make rivers spill over. Dams break apart. An earthquake on the ocean floor can cause a **tsunami**. Huge waves wash over shores during these storms. This type of flooding might only last a few hours. But it is one of the most powerful.

HOW TSUNAMIS FORM

- STARTS WITH AN EARTHQUAKE
- WAVES SPREAD
- HUGE WAVE HITS LAND

FAST AND FORCEFUL

A tsunami can flood miles (kilometers) of coastline in minutes.

FAST AND FORCEFUL

Do the tides cause floods?

FAST AND FORCEFUL

The Moon's pull makes tides rise, which can cause a flood.

Sometimes. The Moon's **gravity** pulls at the Earth. This causes high and low tides twice a day. **Climate change** is making oceans rise. High tides are flooding cities on the coast more often.

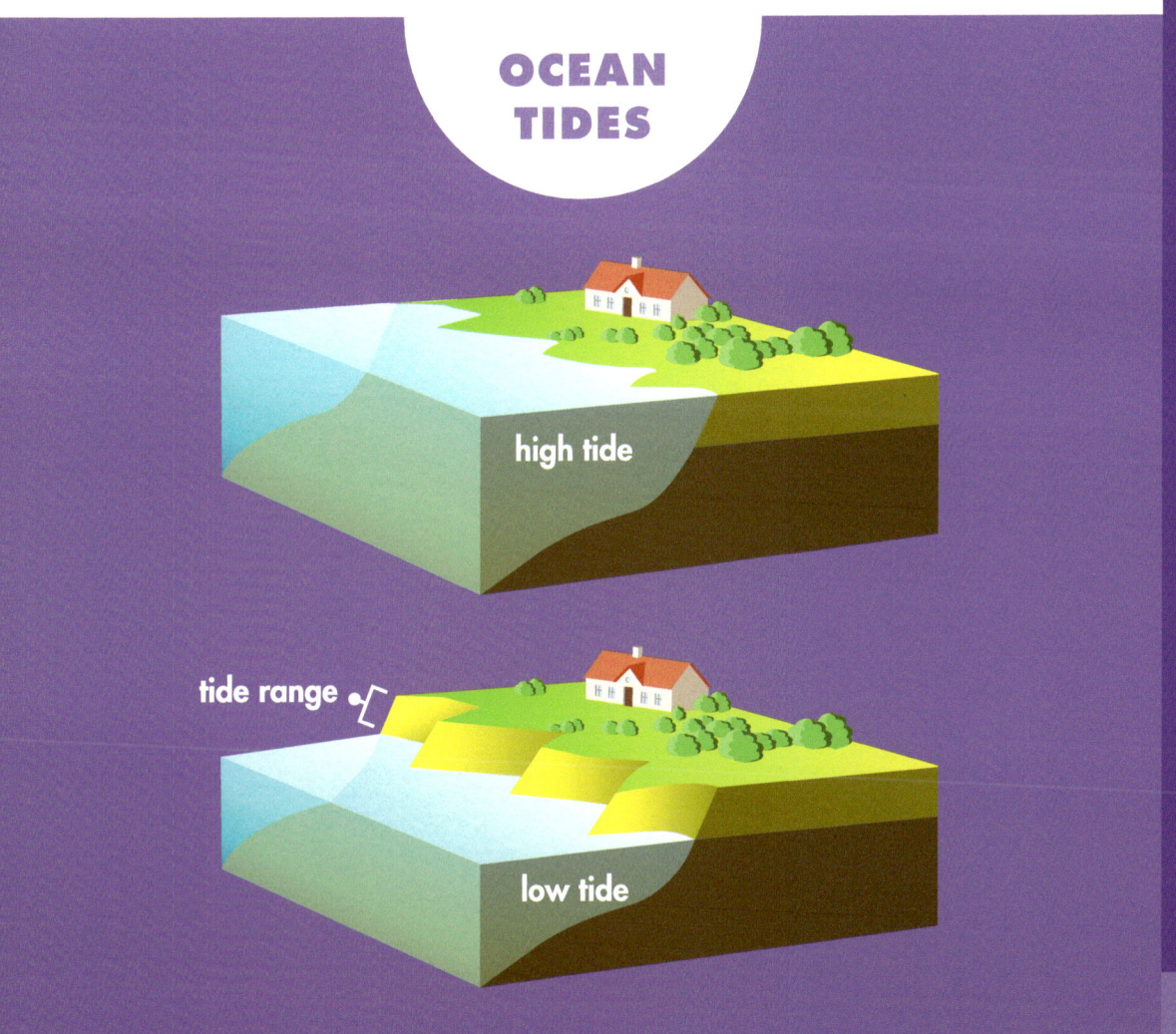

OCEAN TIDES

high tide

tide range

low tide

FAST AND FORCEFUL

What are the dangers of floods?

DID YOU KNOW?
The deadliest US flood happened in Galveston, Texas. In 1900, a hurricane caused a 15-foot (4.6-meter) storm surge that killed more than 8,000 people.

Floodwater is often speedy and strong. Just 6 inches (15 cm) of moving water can knock you over. Flash floods can rip out trees and wash away buildings. Floating **debris** carries deadly force. Floodwater can quickly become **polluted** and unsafe.

Just 2 feet (0.6 m) of water can carry away most cars.

FAST AND FORCEFUL

CHAPTER THREE

Can people prepare for floods?

Most of the time. The National Weather Service (NWS) warns people of major floods. Local weather stations also let people know when flooding is likely. You might need to leave home and move to higher ground. Other times, it is safer to stay where you are.

Rescue teams help people trapped by floodwaters.

WATER WATCHES

FLOOD ALERTS

FLOOD WATCH
Be prepared.
Flooding is possible.

FLOOD ADVISORY
Be aware.
Flooding is likely but minor.

FLOOD WARNING
Take action! A flood is certain or already happening.

FLASH FLOOD WARNING
Take action! Move to higher ground at once.

What should I do in a flood?

WATER WATCHES

Warning signs show where roads may flood during heavy rain.

Move to the upper floor of a building. Listen to the news. **Evacuate** if necessary. Do not drive on flooded streets. Never walk, swim, or drive through floodwater. The rule is "turn around, don't drown!"

1 CLEAN WATER AND CANNED FOOD

2 BATTERIES

3 FLASHLIGHT

4 FIRST AID SUPPLIES

5 WATERPROOF BACKPACK

FLOOD KIT

STAY CURIOUS!

ASK MORE QUESTIONS

Do I live where floods are common?

What if floodwater carries away my car?

Try a BIG QUESTION: Is it safer to leave home during a flood or stay put?

SEARCH FOR ANSWERS

Search the library catalog or the Internet.
A librarian, teacher, or parent can help you.

Using Keywords
Find the looking glass.

Keywords are the most important words in your question.

?

If you want to know about:
- if you live on a floodplain, type: FLOOD MAP FOR (YOUR CITY)
- what to do when trapped in a car, type: FLOOD SAFETY TIPS

LEARN MORE

FIND GOOD SOURCES

Here are some good, safe sources you can use in your research.
Your librarian can help you find more.

Books

Curious about Tsunamis
by Rachel Grack, 2026.

Floods: The Worst in History
by Jenna Vale, 2025.

Internet Sites

Kiddle: Flood Facts for Kids
https://kids.kiddle.co/Flood
Kiddle is an online encyclopedia for kids. Search for facts about floods.

National Geographic Kids: Floods
https://kids.nationalgeographic.com/science/article/flood
National Geographic Kids is an educational website for kids.

Every effort has been made to ensure that these websites are appropriate for children. However, because of the nature of the Internet, it's impossible to guarantee that these sites will remain active indefinitely or that their contents will not be altered.

SHARE AND TAKE ACTION

Pour water over different types of ground to see which ones have the most runoff.

Build flood barriers on a tray. Try sponges, rocks, or mini sandbags. Test with water to see which materials block it the best.

Draw a flood escape route for your house.

GLOSSARY

climate change A human-caused change in the Earth's weather due to warming temperatures.

debris Broken pieces of natural or manmade materials.

dike A long wall built to prevent the flooding of sea water.

evacuate To leave a place of danger and go to a safer place.

gravity The force of a heavenly body that pulls something toward it.

polluted Dirtied with harmful substances.

runoff Water draining off land.

storm surge An abnormal rise of ocean water caused by storms.

tsunami An unusually large sea wave produced by an earthquake or volcanic eruption.

INDEX

alerts, 19
climate change, 15
dams, 4, 7, 12
dangers, 5, 7, 16–17
deadliest floods, 7, 16
earthquakes, 12
flash floods, 8, 9, 10–11, 17, 19
human-made floods, 4, 6–7
Johnstown Flood, 4
safety, 19, 20–21
storm surges, 8, 9, 16
tides, 14–15
tsunamis, 12, 13
types, 8, 9

About the Author

Rachel Grack has been editing and writing children's books since 1999. She lives on a small ranch in the Arizona desert.